MW01178237

Men Should Never...

Men Should Never...

(A How-NOT-to Guide for Today's Man)

by Clare Woodcock and Helena Owen

**Andrews McMeel
Publishing**

Kansas City

Men Should Never . . . copyright © 2005 by The
Manning Partnership Ltd. First published in Great
Britain by The Manning Partnership Ltd © 2003. All
rights reserved. Printed in the United States. No part
of this book may be used or reproduced in any man-
ner whatsoever without written permission except in
the case of reprints in the context of reviews. For
information, write Andrews McMeel Publishing, an
Andrews McMeel Universal company, 4520 Main
Street, Kansas City, Missouri 64111.

05 06 07 08 09 BID 10 9 8 7 6 5 4 3 2 1

ISBN: 0-7407-5044-5

Library of Congress Control Number: 2004111538

Men Should Never...

. . . wear tassels, anywhere.

. . . scream on fairground rides.

. . . miss their mothers when
they're on vacation with the boys.

. . . become clowns.

. . . have smaller thighs than their wives.

. . . be obsessed with sci-fi.

. . . be afraid to travel abroad.

. . . take bowling seriously.

. . . wear their keys on a chain
hanging from their belt loop.

. . . be cautious drivers.

... have a bus pass.

. . . own a compact umbrella.

. . . use a fold-away bicycle.

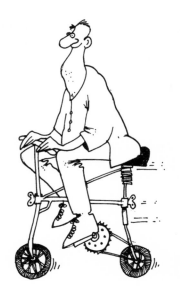

. . . call their mothers "Mommy."

. . . call their wives "Mommy."

. . . rollerskate to
competition standard.

. . . have a gray, black, and red
striped bedspread and
matching wallpaper.

. . . have lace curtains
if they live alone.

. . . use a light-up key ring.

. . . pluck their eyebrows.

. . . eat a sandwich with
a knife and fork.

. . . wear a part in their hair.

. . . fuss about visitors who
wear shoes on their carpets.

. . . have smaller hands than
their wives.

. . . get car sick.

. . . buy wet wipes.

. . . wear large headphones
while listening to a Walkman.

. . . buy themselves cheese
and onion potato chips on their
first date out with you.

. . . press flowers to make their
own greeting cards.

. . . have beaded car seat
covers, unless they
are over sixty.

. . . wear chunky knit sweaters
tucked into jeans.

. . . enjoy watching *Annie*.

. . . have hairless legs.

. . . have visible nose hair.

. . . wear funny ties.

. . . wear funny socks.

. . . wear funny boxer shorts.

. . . buy cute greeting cards
because they like them.

. . . own a small dog.

. . . tell their mothers they are sexy, especially in front of their dads.

. . . use a lunchbox.

. . . wear unbranded jeans.

. . . have blond highlights.

. . . have long toenails
or fingernails.

. . . draw heart-shaped dots
on their i's.

. . . wear tank tops.

. . . enjoy sherry.

. . . say you look like
your mother.

. . . say you act like his mom.

. . . wear high heels.

. . . admit a Nissan Sentra is
their dream car.

. . . customize a station wagon.

. . . play the recorder.

. . . wear dress shoes
with jeans.

. . . call a woman a lesbian
when rejected.

. . . wear multiple
gold necklaces.

. . . get their secretaries to buy
presents for their wives.

... chat about hard drives and RAM to their wives.

. . . wear pants with chunky
plastic zippers.

. . . wear Keds sneakers.

. . . wear any accessory
clipped on their belts.

. . . use a purse.

. . . cry when they see a puppy.

. . . buy a gravy boat to use in
their bachelor pad.

. . . wear a monocle.

. . . have video cameras
set up in their homes.

... try to impress women in bars with the size of their hard drives.

. . . buy scented drawer liners.

. . . buy tissue-box holders.

. . . collect dolls from
around the world.

. . . create their own home-
security systems.

. . . call their wives
the "little woman."

. . . call their wives "the missus."

. . . call their wives "the wife."

... drive VW Beetles.

. . . wear sweatbands as
fashion accessories.

. . . have their own beer glass
at the bar.

. . . wear stockings,
even as a joke.

. . . open a hair salon and name it
after themselves.

... have business meetings
at Denny's.

. . . drink cocktails with
little umbrellas.

... buy *Cosmopolitan.*

. . . book a room at a Motel 6
for an anniversary surprise.

. . . buy satin-padded cards for
their wife's birthday.

. . . tell women to "pipe down."

. . . say, "Look, it's obviously
your time of month,"
during an argument.

. . . refer to women's legs
as "pins."

... have to ask a woman
if she came.

. . . say thank you after sex.

. . . wear a Speedo.

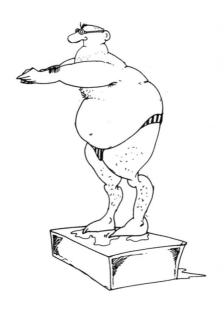

. . . wear socks with sandals.

... decorate their bedrooms
in dusky pink
when they live alone.

. . . wolf down expensive meals.

. . . do the dog paddle.

... wear anything
stonewashed.

. . . commission large studio
photographs of themselves.

. . . have tattoos on their faces,
necks, or hands.

. . . name their children after
their favorite athletes.

. . . name their daughters after
their mothers-in-law.

. . . worry about crow's-feet.

. . . expect gratitude for gifts of
household appliances.

. . . wear the same clothes
as their dads.

... have cushions in the
back of their cars.

. . . dye their hair.

... have the same hairstyles
as their dads.

. . . wear a hairnet.

. . . wear anything displaying
the Gap logo.

. . . take their own candy
to the movie theater.